DOGS

A PORTRAIT OF THE ANIMAL WORLD

Marcus Schneck & Jill Caravan

TODTRI

This book was designed and produced by
TODTRI Book Publishers
Fax : (212) 695-6984
e-mail : info@todtri.com

Printed and bound in Indonesia

ISBN 1-880908-19-0
Visit us on the web!
www.todtri.com

Authors: Marcus Schneck & Jill Caravan

Publisher: Robert M. Tod
Book Designer: Mark Weinberg
Editor: Mary Forsell
Photo Editor: Natasha Milne
Design Associate: Jackie Skroczky
Typesetting: Command-O, NYC

INTRODUCTION

The beagle was probably developed in the sixteenth century by crossings between the harrier and ancient English hounds. It is affectionate, clean, tranquil, and pleasing, with a harmonious voice.

They can be seen walking along our city parks, romping or tied in backyards, wandering stray in search of food, napping in our living rooms, begging at our tables—just about anywhere in society.

In most places, they are known as the family dog, having become part of our families throughout the world. But it was not always so. If they are all dogs, why do they look so different, and where did they all come from?

It is estimated that there are 150 million members of the canine population in the world, members of the family Canidae. Most of them are domestic dogs, members of the species Canis familiaris.

Even among C. familiaris, *there is great variability, resulting in more than 300 breeds throughout the world—from the Great Dane at 150 pounds (67.5 kilograms) and 32 inches (80 centimetres) high (to the shoulder) to the Chihuahua at 1.5 pounds (.68 kilogram) and 6 inches (15 centimetres) high. They also vary in function and other physical characteristics.*

Archaeologists have found evidence of dogs on earth twenty–five to thirty million years ago. The creature called Cynodesmus evolved into a wolflike animal named Tomarctus, which evolved into the ancestor of the wolf, the jackal, the fox, the coyote, and all the canines. Let us examine the dog's habits and history.

PACK BEHAVIOUR

One of the things all canines have in common is their instinctive behaviour as pack animals.

A pack is a group of animals that live together all dependent on one another for protection, companionship, mates, babysitters for the young, and hunting companions.

Each pack has a leader, the most dominant male, and other members of the pack are followers. Some of the followers rank higher than others, but none are as esteemed as the leader.

The leader is probably the only male to mate, usually with the most dominant female. When they have pups, the female becomes the leader of the pack until the pups are old enough to travel and hunt with the pack.

The most important reason for a pack is hunting. Canines are not fast enough to outrun some prey, so they have joined together so they can circle the prey and then attack.

After the kill, the leader eats first, followed by other members of the pack in their hierarchical order. Older canines unable to get their own food are given food by other members of the pack, and the leader may even take food to his mate while she is raising the pups in the den. Pups are fed by the mother as well as by other adults in the group. They lick food from the adults' lips or eat what the adults have regurgitated for them.

After eating the pack rests awhile and

The Irish wolfhound was used by the ancient Celts for hunting wolves and was later brought to Ireland by the Romans. It is still used for hunting stags, wild boar, wolves, and coyotes and can kill a man by grabbing him by the throat.

One theory about the weimaraner is that it is the fruit of crossings overseen by Grand Duke Karl August of Weimar between a regular pointer and a certain yellow pointer.

The cairn terrier was developed in Scotland to seek out animals that invaded small mounds of stones, called 'cairns', that were used to mark property boundaries or graves.

The Labrador retriever is a short, solid dog approximately 22 inches (55.8 centimetres) high and weighing 55 to 75 pounds (25 to 34 kilograms). Sometimes a yellow pup appears in an otherwise black litter.

may spend some time playing. If there is more food in the area, the pack may stay in the area awhile. If not, the leader decides when the pack moves on.

If some members have strayed or been separated from the pack during hunting or play, the canines will howl to gather the pack together.

The male leader remains so until it is unseated by a more dominant dog or dies.

DOMESTICATION

It is believed that the ancestor of the domestic dog—the wolf—was the first canine welcomed into the life of man about twelve thousand or more years ago, largely because of its pack instinct and hunting skills.

Cave dwellers probably offered the dog food and protection in exchange for use of its keen hunting instincts and a different kind of protection.

People who lived in a type of family group probably threw scraps to hungry animals hovering around. The wolves soon realized that man had hunting skills of his own (weapons) and began treating him as leader when permitted.

After a while, man began to take interest in the wolves and their cubs, maybe even adopting some and treating them as members of their own family 'pack'. Over time, these wolves probably took part in man's hunts, flushing and isolating the prey for man to kill.

In 1350 the various English spaniels were divided into seven breeds: the clumber, the Sussex, the Welsh springer, the English springer, the field, the Irish water, and the cocker, shown here.

The Chihuahua is the oldest breed on the American continents and the smallest breed in the world. Although native to Mexico (its name is that of a Mexican state), it was introduced by the Chinese.

8

Crossing the bulldog with the Old English terrier and adding Spanish pointer blood resulted in the bullterrier. It was used to guard flocks, hunt mice, and be a companion and guard dog.

DOG LORE

What we know of dogs from physiological evidence has been backed up by what man passed on about his relationships with and beliefs about dogs.

Prehistoric painters began depicting the jackal and the hyena around 4500 B.C., first in the act of helping a hunter. The handle of a knife estimated to be almost five thousand years old is inscribed with the outline of a dog with a collar, taken to be proof that dogs were also used as guards.

In Egypt, tombs were raised and fearful epigraphs were written to deceased dogs. Killing and even being cruel to a dog were punishable by death.

The Persians, too, considered killing a dog a crime. They even declared the dog 'guardian of the herds and protector of man'.

The Greeks said the dog was forged by Vulcan and expressed its role in mythology on pottery and sculpture as well as in literature.

In pre–Columbian cultures the dog was also considered supernatural; after a man's death, his canine was killed and buried with him.

The German short-haired pointer is descended from the Spanish pointer, which was introduced into Germany in 1600 by Flemish hunters. Crossings with the Italian pointer made it faster and more energetic.

In the past, the English cocker spaniel was employed as a marvelous finder of game. Its name comes from that of the woodcock.

Like its larger brothers, the giant and standard schnauzers, the miniature schnauzer is descended from ancient terriers, but it also carries in its veins the blood of the affenpinscher.

The Komondor is descended from Tibetan dogs and was brought to Hungary one thousand years ago. It has been used with outstanding results as a police dog in snowy regions.

The Hebrews, however, did not think so highly of the canine species. In the Old Testament, the dog was a pariah—dirty and emaciated, eating garbage in the roads.

It was not much better in the Orient. Three centuries before Christ, dog meat was popular on the menus of aristocrats.

In the Middle Ages, dogs were used to 'cure' man's ills. It was believed that the blood of a white dog would calm madness and the blood of a black dog would ease a painful childbirth.

In seventeenth–century Europe, exchanges, sales, and contests among the various European states led to respect for the dog, which was commonly depicted by painters lying at the feet of its most genteel patrons.

Among the famous painters who depicted them are Durer, Botticelli, Piero della Francesca, Mantegna, Titian, Bosch, Brueghel the Elder, Rubens, Canaletto, Velazquez, and Goya.

Poetry and theatre also resounded with love of the dog, including works by Lorenzo de Medici and Shakespeare.

The Boston terrier was developed through long breeding of the bulldog, the French bulldog, the bullterrier, and the boxer.

BREEDS

Prior to the classical period, the Greeks had wolf dogs. The philosopher Aristotle listed the various breeds of dog, giving them names of the countries from which they came. Thus, in 300 B.C. there were dogs from Cyrenaica, India, Egypt, and Epirus. But history has not recorded what was different about each.

Ever since prehistoric times, new types of dogs and breeds similar to those today came about by natural mutation as well as by crossing masterminded by man.

As new breeds were developed, they were classified according to their uses: hunting, guarding, shepherding, warring, racing and combating, rescuing, working, companioning, and guiding. Each is discussed in the following pages.

While the foxhound, which comes in many colours, appears to be docile and calm, it can expend a great deal of energy while on the trail of its prey.

Hunting Dogs

Throughout history, dogs have played a role in civilisations wherever there has been hunting or conflict. Spaniels, retrievers, terriers, hounds, setters, and beagles are some of the types of dogs that have been used for hunting throughout the centuries. Lesser–known hunting dogs include the boxer, the greyhound, the puli, and the Samoyed.

The English springer spaniel is the founder of all the English hunting spaniels. The Welsh springer spaniel, pictured, is a little smaller. It is always red and white.

Native to Newfoundland, the Labrador retriever was first brought to Great Britain in 1800 by English ships coming from Labrador.

The bluetick coonhound was developed through crossings among various hounds, especially for the hunting of raccoons.

The golden retriever makes a pleasant and quiet family dog, but needs a large apartment or house and, if possible, a yard.

In Rome, hunting dogs were held in high esteem. The Latin poet Ovid gave instructions on ensuring good pups. The writer said people should not trust dogs fed on scraps because they would become accustomed to licking blood and end up attacking live animals.

The Greek Oppian, author of *Cynegetica*, in his turn was personally involved in breeding small dogs he considered to be most adapted to hunting in the woods.

It was during the Middle Ages that the first true specialisation of hunting dogs began. Pointers and setters searched for prey, while hounds flushed stag; greyhounds were used for following, the Molossus for attacking, beaver dogs for burrowing.

The dog became extremely important in the sporting life. Already there were essays on dog care, recommending that men keep the packs warm when they return from the hunt and keep their wooden feeding bowls clean.

The foremost country for hunting dogs in the seventeentn century was France. All

Bred near the border between England and Scotland for driving out foxes, the Border terrier was also used for hunting martens.

The Brittany spaniel is a lively French breed, characterized by a short tail and slightly fringed chest. It was traditionally used as a bird dog.

The golden retriever was probably developed through crossings of the bloodhound with unspecified golden–coated dogs belonging to a Russian circus that visited England in the midnineteenth century.

The setter, as its name indicates, takes a half–sitting stance to indicate the presence of game to the hunter. The English setter, shown here, has a silky, moderately long coat.

The Irish setter is probably older than the English setter. Their common ancestor, however, is the Spanish pointer.

the Kings Louis loved hunting, and they knew how to go about it with royal majesty. Stag and fox hunts became worldly events with a great deal of staging.

Great and noble breeds such as the Chiens Blancs de Roi, the Grand Bleu de Gascogne, the Poitevin, and the Chien d'Artois were developed. They worked in packs accompanied by horns and rows of huntsmen, beaters, and horsemen.

In the nineteenth century, the great dog packs of the nobility disappeared, but middle–class hunters kept one or two dogs, usually pointers and setters.

Dogs were naturally hounds, with instincts for finding game, flushing it out, and driving it into open terrain for the

hunter to capture.

Man also taught the dog to 'stand'—stop suddenly, with one paw lifted, the moment it senses game. The stand signals to the hunter that the game is in the direction the dog is facing.

Because game sometimes run away only wounded after being hit by ammunition, man also taught the dog to retrieve. Retrievers specialise in recovering game that has been hit from wherever it may run to or fall.

Man also developed the terrier into an expert at flushing game from its den. The aggressive terrier, with its short legs and dangerous teeth, penetrates the tunnels made by animals like foxes, badgers, and weasels.

The Scottish terrier
was developed in
Scotland in 1700,
but until 1890 it
was known as the
Aberdeen terrier,
after the town in
which it was raised.

Descended from the bloodhound and the foxhound, the black–and–tan coonhound was developed in the United States on the basis of its colours.

The pointer was developed two centuries ago by crossings among the Italian pointer, the foxhound, the bloodhound, the greyhound, the Newfoundland, the setter, and the bulldog. Its name suggests its stance when in the presence of game.

Guard Dogs

From ancient times, dogs have had other skills besides hunting. Among their more valuable latent instincts has been that of guarding.

During the Middle Ages, dogs were raised at monasteries, sometimes as companion dogs, but also for protection. The bloodhound, for example, was created by the monks at the abbey of St. Hubert in the Belgian Ardennes. The German shepherd originated from breeding by German monks who wanted a dog to protect the monastery from bandits.

In ancient Greece, some dogs, probably descended from the Molossus, the grandfather of all guard dogs (with its great size and aggressiveness), were used to guard sacred places. Legend holds that one particular dog followed for 21 miles (33.6 kilometres) and captured a thief who had robbed the Temple of Aphrodite.

The modern guard dog is the result of specialised breeding and must be trained to overcome obstacles in its path, to attack people without injuring them, to ignore gunshots, to refuse food from strangers, to run great distances, and to keep calm.

Police work is a common area for guard dogs to be used, with breeds such as the German shepherd, the Belgian shepherd, the Doberman, the

The mastiff is descended from the Tibetan mastiff, which was introduced into Europe by the Phoenicians.

Gifted with the finest sense of smell, the bloodhound has been used to unearth small game and find lost people, buried miners, and hidden treasure.

Incised on some Greek money dating back to 36 B.C. is the image of a dog very similar to the Great Dane of today. It is known as the 'Apollo of Dogs'.

The rottweiler is probably descended from the Italian mastiff and was used during the Middle Ages as a herd dog.

Airedale, the giant schnauzer, the rottweiler, the bloodhound, and the Labrador retriever.

Training begins during the dog's first year, and it serves for the next seven or eight years, sometimes retiring with a 'pension' from the force. Guard dogs for homes are also trained in schools for several months.

Not everyone needs a commissioned officer to guard his home. Many companion dogs, once they learn that they are part of their human animal pack, can defend their masters' homes simply by barking loudly enough to scare away any potential intruders.

The female Doberman is tranquil, sensitive, and affectionate with the family, but suspicious of strangers. The male is extremely intelligent, but impetuous, and needs an energetic master.

The Belgian sheepdog was isolated in 1891 by Professor Reul of the Belgian faculty of veterinary sciences. He recognized three main types: long haired, short haired, and shaggy haired.

Shepherd Dogs

Certain breeds of dog have been bred especially to protect livestock from predators, while at the same time not harming the livestock themselves. These are known as shepherd dogs or sheepdogs.

Herd dogs first appeared thousands of years ago in the service of nomadic shepherds in Asia because of the threat of wild animals. Early sheepdogs were big and courageous, ready to go for the throat of bears, wolves, or any other intruders.

Phoenician merchants then brought them to Europe, where they mated with local dogs and developed into numerous famous breeds. They were preferred to have white coats, so they could be seen easily at

night and were distinguishable from the dark-coloured bears and wolves. This explains why there are today such light-coated sheepdogs as the Kuvasz, the Maremmano–Abruzzese, the Tatra, the Great Pyrenees, and the Bergamasco.

Other good candidates are the German shepherd, the Belgian shepherd, the Norwegian hound, the collie, the bobtail, and the corgi. Some of these, however, have been bred more for defence than shepherding in modern times.

In England there are still competitions just for sheepdogs, who must be able to find 10 sheep placed 800 metres (2,640 feet, or .5 mile) away and herd them into an enclosure. The dog should work silently,

*A hardy, agile, untiring sheepdog,
the Border collie is said to have
an eye that can hypnotise livestock.*

The Norwegian elkhound is specialised in hunting elk, which it can scent from a distance of several kilometres.

For as long as man has kept sheep and needed a guardian to defend them, the Maremmano sheepdog has been in existence.

The Shetland sheepdog is probably descended from collies brought to the Scottish island of Shetland and crossed with the Yakkin, a small island dog now no longer recognised, brought over in the boats of fishermen.

with concentration and speed. It may not attack or bite the sheep.

Besides herding sheep and cows, the sheepdog should be able to herd geese, ducks, hens, and domestic rabbits without any of the temptations of hunger. Only in the last century, when the menace of bears and wolves has become less likely, has the sheepdog been mostly given the job of finding lost animals and returning them to the fold.

The best candidate for a sheepdog is a good–natured puppy who can be paired with an old herding dog.

War Dogs

Since very early times the dog has also been used in war as sentinels, messengers and scouts; to carry munitions, medicine, and telephone equipment; and to locate mines and find the injured.

Some of the types of dogs that were most commonly used for hunting throughout the ages are the German shepherd, the Bouvier des Flandres, and the briard.

The Romans, for example, used dogs as

The Border collie is descended from reindeer-herding dogs brought to Scotland by the Viking invaders. These dogs were later crossed with the Valee sheepdog.

The Pembroke corgi is the short–tailed version of the Welsh corgi. The medium–long–tailed corgi is the Cardigan.

The collie (also called rough collie) has long been an outstanding sheepdog. The name comes from 'colley', the black–faced, black–footed Scottish sheep that collies guarded.

The briard has been known for some centuries and was used as a sentry dog during World War I. Some briards have retained their ancient shepherding and guarding instincts.

Herding cows is the true mission of the Bouvier des Flandres, formed by crossing the Griffon and the Beauceron. It has also been used as a guard dog and for rescuing the wounded in battle.

message carriers and attack dogs. For attack and defence, the Molossus, with its pincer-like fangs, was equipped with iron collars bristling with blades. In the face of such an apparition, the enemy was often put to flight before the battle was joined.

The most unfortunate animals were the so-called messenger dogs. The military orders were put in a small copper tube that the dog was forced to swallow. Because of the urgency involved, the receiver of the message would not wait for the tube to be expelled naturally; instead he would slaughter the messenger.

Modern armies have always preferred their own national breeds. Thus they have used the German shepherd, the collie, the Doberman, and the rottweiler. Breeds with white coats are avoided since they are easily spotted by the enemy.

During World War I, dogs were armed with gas masks. In World War II, Germany had an army of 200,000 trained dogs guarding the Nazi concentration camps. The Americans used dogs mostly in the conquest of the Japanese–held Pacific islands, to flush out snipers and search for wounded in the jungles.

The Soviets trained dogs to expect food under ammunition wagons. They then put TNT charges on the backs of the poor hungry dogs and sent them toward the enemy, exploding the charges as the dogs advanced.

Following page:

The greyhound was probably descended from the Arab greyhound, the Sloughi, which was brought to Europe by the Phoenicians. It was used to hunt deer and boar because it could catch them and pull them down without stopping.

The whippet was developed at the end of the nineteenth century by crossing greyhounds, Italian greyhounds, and the terrier. Although it is also a companion dog, it is used at the track for short races and can reach a speed of 37 miles (59 kilometres) per hour.

The French bulldog is a native French breed, possibly with some English bull-dog blood. A companion dog and a guard dog, it is also a ruthless hunter of mice.

Racing and Combat Dogs

Less noble endeavours include the use of canines for racing and combat. Dog races were organised as far back as pre–Roman Gaul. In these events, dogs are raced on dog tracks and spectators bet on the results, as in horse races.

In sixteenth century England, rules were established, organising societies were founded, tracks were built, and dogs were bred for their racing abilities. Two of those breeds are the greyhound and the whippet, both still known today for their speed and grace.

At first, racing dogs were led by a real hare, and the first dog to capture the prey was the winner. Because animal lovers protested, the first mechanical rabbit was constructed in 1876.

The mechanism was perfected in the early 1900s by an American engineer, Owen Smith, causing much growth in the sport. Even today, some Anglo–Saxon and Spanish countries still use a live rabbit. But for the most part, race dogs today chase mechanical rabbits on sand tracks for as long as 1,000 metres (3,300 feet). Training a racing dog begins when the dog is approximately nine months old. It takes approximately another nine months before the dog is ready to race.

The ideal racing dog should not weigh more than 13.6 pounds (6 kilograms) and must be able to run 400 metres (1,320 feet) in 22 seconds.

Throughout history, organised combat between dogs and dogs and between dogs and wild animals took place practically everywhere.

Combats took place in the amphitheatres of ancient Rome between dogs and tigers, dogs and lions, and dogs and dogs. Most often used was Molossus, a beast weighing more than 170 pounds (76.6 kilograms).

In Britain, powerful combat dogs known as Pugnaces Britanniae were raised and sold even overseas. The bulldog, for example, is an English dog bred to fight bulls. Its nose is pugged so it can breathe even when it has the bull tightly by the throat.

The first country to prohibit combat between animals by law was Holland in 1689, followed 150 years later by France and England. Even in modern times, however, such sport takes place in many places without approval by the law.

43

Rescue Dogs

Probably the most famous rescue dog is the St. Bernard, often pictured with a cask of brandy around its neck for grateful mountain climbers injured by avalanches.

For three hundred years, these big dogs, raised by the Cenobite Brothers in the Hospice of St. Bernard in Switzerland, have been used to find lost people. They are the result of crossings between German Great Danes and Newfoundlands.

Rescues attributed to St. Bernards number in the thousands, and the story of one particular St. Bernard, Barry, has become a legend. Barry apparently saved forty–four people from the snow and was then killed by the forty–fifth, who mistook him for a bear. The irony is that the name Barry comes from *bari,* which in German means 'little bear'. A statue is dedicated to Barry in Paris, and for years the St. Bernard was also known as 'Barryhund'.

The St. Bernard, however, is not the only dog ever used for rescue work. The first rescue dogs (of the Molossian type) were used centuries ago for tracing paths that disappeared in snowstorms. Today, the dog most preferred for rescue work after avalanches and earthquakes is the German shepherd. The most popular breed for water rescues is the Newfoundland.

The Samoyed is a classic sled dog, able to pull heavy loads long distances. Its coat remains white naturally without periodic baths.

Working Dogs

Many dogs have also been classified as working dogs even though their tasks were not hunting, shepherding, rescuing, or other more traditional endeavours.

Until 1500, dogs were trained to pull carts loaded with heavy goods. Eventually laws were passed prohibiting excessive exploitation in this manner.

Dogs have turned the wheels of the mills in Scotland and the butter churns in Wales; they have operated spits in Central Europe and the 'sacred wheels' of monks of the Far East. In Holland and Denmark, German shepherds are used to detect small leaks in gas pipes, even underground. In times of poor hygiene, dogs were used to draw off parasites, and even warmed their masters' bodies.

The spitz dogs are a distinctive group that all have an erect tail, a wolflike face, and a ruff of fur around the neck. They all originated in the far north, where the cold weather seems to have been instrumental in preserving their distinctive appearance.

The Alaskan malamute is a Nordic dog, descended from the Arctic wolf. Its name comes from Malemute, an Alaskan tribe.

Sled dogs are sometimes the only means of crossing great areas of frozen land. Teams of Alaskan malamutes, for example, have participated in polar expeditions of Roald Amundsen (1872 to 1928) and the Duke of the Abruzzi, also known as Luigi Amedeo (1873 to 1933). Only with the sleds pulled by these dogs was it possible to carry supplies to villages.

In arctic countries, sled dogs such as the Eskimo are hitched to the sleds either in a fan–shaped formation or in pairs side by side. The Eskimos and the Siberians also use different methods of yoking.

In Alaska, sled–pulling contests are very popular. In Anchorage, Alaskan malamutes compete periodically over courses 500 miles (800 kilometres) long.

Another job—finding truffles in certain areas of Italy and France—was done by specially trained dogs. The truffle is a rare, delicious, and expensive mushroomlike fungus that grows on oak tree roots. The search for them is conducted only with mongrels or terriers that do not allow themselves to become distracted by small game. Dogs such as terriers, bassets, and schnauzers have also been used to catch mice in food stores.

In modern times, dogs are used (and often abused) in medical research, to entertain in circuses, and to 'act' in movies and on television. They even preceded man into space.

The basset hound is descended directly from the bloodhound. Shakespeare said it has 'ears which sweep away the morning dew'.

The standard schnauzer comes from Bavaria, but the date of its origin is not known. The name comes from the German word schnauze, meaning 'muzzle'.

Companion Dogs

As the Middle Ages progressed, affection for the dog grew. By the beginning of the Renaissance, owning a beautiful dog even had snob appeal. Hunting was still practised, but it was also considered pleasing to have a walking dog and a companion dog. It was a status symbol to go out accompanied by a Molossus and to attend one of the races featuring the greyhound.

Many companion dogs popular today come from working breeds: the poodle, a former pointing breed and water dog; the dalmatian and fox terrier, former hunting breeds; and the collie, a former sheepdog.

The traditional companion dog is medium-sized, small, or miniature. To make the so-called toy breeds more appealing, some

The wirehaired fox terrier has been called the well-dressed brother of the smooth fox terrier. It has a coat that is dense, shaggy, and compact without excessive curling.

There is total disagreement concerning the origin of the dalmatian. In 1700 a dog known as the Bengal pointer, similar to the dalmatian, existed in England, calling into question the dalmatian's Yugoslavian origins.

The standard poodle is one of three types of poodles; the other two are the miniature and the toy.

breeders have bred them to weigh as little as 2.5 pounds (1.1 kilograms).

Of course, today most dogs are brought into the home as companions, becoming members of their families no matter what their size or ancestry.

Guide Dogs

The ultimate companion dogs are those trained to serve people who are physically challenged by vision or hearing impairment or some other physical disability.

The first centres for training arose in France and Germany in 1915. They were designed to help soldiers returning from the front with impaired vision. Other centres followed immediately all over the world.

The German shepherd became the preferred dog for this training. Good results have also been achieved with the Belgian shepherd, the Labrador, the boxer, and the collie.

Female dogs are preferred for their greater docility and obedience. Male dogs are too likely to become distracted by a bitch in heat.

In recent decades, dogs have been trained to alert hearing-impaired people to noises or danger in their environment and to assist people confined to wheelchairs.

The boxer is a very good–natured and loyal dog. It doesn't bear grudges and is particularly affectionate with children.

The German shepherd is ideal for people like policemen, guards, and others who enjoy training and working with their dogs.

The Brittany spaniel has earned great popularity among millions of hunters because of its moderate size, which allows them to transport it easily. Because of its jovial character, it is also popular as a companion dog.

The saluki is probably the fruit of ancient crossings among Egyptian and Asiatic greyhounds. It bears the name of an ancient Arab city, Salug, and is considered a sacred gift of Allah.

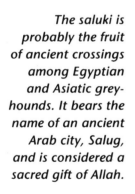

DOG SHOWS

Once certain dogs were bred for various purposes, people began to expect particular characteristics in those dogs. Breeders quickly set to work to fulfill those demands. From there, it was only a brief jump to competitions among breeders to decide who had the most success in specialised breeding.

The first dog show took place in 1859 in the town hall of Newcastle upon Tyne in England. It was for hunting dogs only, and fifty pointers and setters took part.

Standards and genealogy, the stuff of which today's dog shows are made, did not play a role. More than anything, it played itself out as a sporting event without regulations.

Fourteen years later, on April 1, 1873, the English Kennel Club was founded in London. Later, the *Studbook*, which is today known as the *Book of Origins*, was begun to record data about the breeds. The American Kennel Club (AKC) was then formed in 1884 and the Italian Kennel Club in 1898.

The first dog shows in the United States

Most probably the long–haired dachshund was developed by crossing the short–haired dachshund with some sort of spaniel. It differs from the short–haired variety only by its softer and longer coat.

Crossings among the Skye terrier, the black–and–tan toy terrier, the Dandie Dinmont, and the Maltese all contributed to the makeup of the Yorkshire terrier, developed to catch rats in mine shafts.

55

Popular in Italy during the Renaissance, the papillon was perfected by French breeders. It is also called the butterfly dog because of its wide, erect ears. Papillon, of course, means 'butterfly' in French.

date back to 1875. While only fifty dogs were entered then, it is common to have as many as seven thousand in today's shows.

By the end of the 1800s, the animal lovers' movement in England had begun to combat animal abuse. In 1898, docking of dogs' ears was abolished in England, and dogs whose ears were cut were not allowed into dog shows. The practice is not allowed in American dog shows, either, except for surgery required by some breeds to the tips of the ears. It should be done by a veterinarian when the dog is about three months old and the ear cartilage is consistent.

Breeds have been classified into groups, which may vary from country to country. The AKC recognizes more than 130 breeds in 7 different groups: sporting, hound, working, terrier, toy, nonsporting, and herding.

Standards for each breed are established by committees elected by members of various kennel clubs specialising in each breed. In the United States, these standards must be approved by the AKC and give weight, height, colour coat, and type.

Issued since 1929, today's standards represent an ideal dog and are used as guides

The cocker spaniel is not so reliable as a watchdog because once its hunting instincts are awakened, as by the scent of a wild animal, all its obedience training is forgotten.

for breeders and dog show judges in evaluating the quality of each dog. Using these standards and keeping in mind the dog's unique sensory, communicative, and pack characteristics, breeders have been able to develop breeds with the best of these traits.

Other classifying organisations through out the world include the United Kennel Club (UKC), The Kennel Club of Great Britain (TKC), the Canadian Kennel Club (CKC), and the Federation Cynologique Internationale (FCI) world registry.

SENSES

No matter how much man tries to domesticate the dog, all one has to do is to watch a dog for a few minutes to note the extent to which it is still really a wild animal. We sometimes tend to forget that because dogs have learned to some degree to temper their wildness.

But they still retain all the physical attributes that would allow them to survive in the wild if they had never been domesticated.

For example, the muscle structure of the dog is much the same its wolf ancestor, allowing the animal to jump, run, stalk, and engage in battle. The dog's jaw is powerful enough to bite through a human limb, yet most dogs keep their bite in check unless truly provoked by teasing or abuse.

And even though they are fed and protected by humans, their senses and other instincts are still strong enough to detect danger and prey.

The Jack Russell terrier was developed in the last century by an English clergyman, Parson Jack Russell, a great breeder and well-known dog lover.

The Airedale terrier was developed about a century ago in the county of York by crossing the ancient working terrier and the otter hound. Its name comes from the river Aire in Yorkshire.

The bloodhound, more than one thousand years old, was created by the monks of St. Hubert in Belgium.

The English bulldog descended from the ancient Asiatic mastiff. The word 'bulldog' refers to its robust look and the power with which it attacked bulls in arena combat.

The Eskimo dog is native to eastern Siberia and was introduced into Alaska and Greenland in the nineteenth century. A team of twenty Eskimo dogs can pull a sled carrying a 2-ton (1.8-metric-ton) load for 25 miles (40 kilometres) without stopping. It does not bark, but howls like a wolf.

shepherds, 200 million. Some experts have said that the dog's sense of smell is some five hundred times greater than man's.

To illustrate: Dogs can detect a drop of blood in 10.5 pints (5 litres) of water. They can differentiate between the smells of various animals. They can smell meat, drugs, and other contraband through plastic bags and luggage. The can distinguish the odours of various people. And they can follow the tracks of animals even hours later or when they have been deliberately disguised.

The dog's mouth is just as important as its nose, with a well-developed sense of taste closely linked to its sense of smell. The tongue is used for lapping water, eating food, cleaning the body, licking wounds, feeling objects, and expressing affection.

The canine's forty-two teeth, whose position and bite vary from breed to breed, are often evident when a dog pants. Since dogs do not perspire, they must pant to cool the body down after exercise or during periods of hot weather.

The dog's hearing is the next most sensitive sense. The same sound that a man can barely hear at 13 feet (3.9 metres) a dog can hear at more than 80 feet (24 metres). It can also differentiate similar sounds, such as its master's car from other cars on the block. It can even pick up ultrasonic vibrations, which are of the highest frequency.

Although it is not their best sense, dogs' vision is also quite good. Some say dogs see only in black and white, but other experiments have shown that they may see some

The most important of dogs senses, especially to hunting dogs, is the sense of smell. In man, olfactory cells cover a total area of about .64 square inch (4 square centimetres); in a German shepherd, they cover 24 square inches (156 square centimetres). Man has approximately 5 million olfactory cells; basset hounds, 125 million; fox terriers, 150 million; and German

The Cavalier King Charles spaniel has the same rootstock as the English toy spaniel and has noteworthy senses of smell and vision.

colours, mostly pastel.

Experts do agree, however, that dogs see better at night. This is because of a light–reflecting layer at the back of the eye, which acts as an intensifying device and enables them to make optimum use of existing light. It is this reflection that seems to make their eyes glow in the dark.

Their field of vision, too, is better than man's. Man's is 180 degrees; that of dogs is up to 250 degrees. This helps in making their eyes more sensitive to movement, making up for their lack of vision in detail.

Touch is not so important to the daily survival of a dog, but it is certainly at least equal to that of human beings. Dogs can feel when you pet or caress them, when you discipline them with newspaper, or accidentally step on their paws, as well as when they step on a sharp object or get bitten hard by a parasite such as a flea.

Some say dogs have still another sense—a mysterious sixth sense that allows them to find their way home after being dumped off by an abusive owner or to predict by a howl in the middle of the night someone in the family has died.

INTELLIGENCE AND TRAINING

Dogs probably aren't as supernatural as some people think they are. But then how intelligent are they? Current thinking on the subject is that the average dog is as intelligent as a human four–year–old. But trainers generally agree that the true tests of intelligence are how much they remember and how quickly they can learn new tasks.

Most dogs can remember where their food and water are located, where you want them to defecate and urinate, where they sleep, and who are members of the household. Don't think that the dog is sitting there remembering things all the time. These things are the result of associative memory, so the dog remembers, for example, where its food is located only when it gets hungry and 'decides' to eat.

Most dogs also understand some words and signals. This may vary by breed, but almost any dog should be able to master some basic rules and commands. Training can start the day you bring your puppy home, but don't expect any real results until the dog is three to six months old or older.

When a dog comes into your family, you take care of all its needs: food, protection,

health, play, and maybe a mate. Because it is naturally looking for a leader, you take the place of the leader of the wild pack.

Dogs are happiest when they know exactly where they stand. If they have come to accept a human leader, they will welcome the decisions and commands from the leader and the order you bring to their lives. In fact, most of pack life is devoted to reinforcing each animal's particular position in the pack, even if it turns out to be lowly.

Just as there are basics in life that humans need to learn to be accepted in society, so are there rules for dogs to learn before they can be acceptable to the family and society. After an

In the Middle Ages, the dalmatian was used as a hound. Later it became a 'carriage dog', following its master whether on foot, on horseback, or in a carriage.

The ideal age for the first mating of a male dog is eighteen months. For the female, wait until the second or third heat so the uterus will have reached adult proportions. It is likely that proper mating practices produced these golden retriever puppies.

The English springer spaniel is used to hunt over all types of terrain, even that thick with brambles.

owner has established him– or herself as the leader of the pack in the dog's mind, the dog will be conducive to learning these things.

Another basic principle to remember is reward and punishment: When the dog does what it is supposed to do, it should be lavished with praise, petted, given a treat, or rewarded in some way it prefers. When it does not do what it is being told to do, it should hear a loud 'No' or some other noise that will deter it.

Hitting a dog is not the best way to discipline it. With most dogs, it breeds fear into the dog, and the dog associates the pain of being hit with the person who hit it, not with what it wasn't supposed to be doing.

It is also inadvisable to punish a dog for something hours or even a few minutes after the incident. If the dog makes a mess on the carpet while you are out, just clean it up and don't reprimand the dog. If you tell the dog 'No' while it is sitting there watching you, it will think you don't want it to sit there and watch you. Punishment must take place immediately after or during the incident so the dog associates the punishment with the deed.

Dog trainers recommend that one always use

The ancient Maltese was developed in Italy with the addition of miniature spaniel and poodle blood. It does not shed like other dogs in fall and spring.

The Pekingese probably has spitz blood. It was brought to Europe in 1860 by British and French soldiers who found the dogs in the ruins of the Summer Palace.

the same command and the same gestures and that training time be made fun for the dog as well as educational. It is also advisable to use a firm voice for commands; a soft, high voice for praise; and a deep, harsh voice for punishment.

Housebreaking

Housebreaking is the first thing most people want their dog to learn. Puppies cannot be expected to learn this until they are three months old, but training can still begin as soon as the puppy comes home.

Until that time, most puppies lived with littermates in a pen, where they relieved themselves anywhere they wanted to. Now the puppy must be taught that there are rules.

One place the puppy will not go is where it sleeps and eats, a phenomenon called the 'denning instinct'. It is best to use this by keeping the dog in a crate (which it will consider its den) and removing it only when you want to take it outdoors to relieve itself at regular intervals. After a few weeks, the dog learns to wait to relieve itself until it goes outside.

Leash

Puppies need to get used to wearing a collar and leash. This can be done by putting the leash on the dog in the house and letting it walk around and get accustomed to the idea. This is much more effective than waiting until it's time to take the dog out and then expecting it to be comfortable with a leash.

Barking

Most owners don't want their dogs to bark excessively or while the family is out of the house. To avoid this, whenever the dog barks, the owner must respond with a loud 'No'.

Sometimes an owner must trick the dog into believing he or she has left the house to discover this behaviour and discipline it.

Other Behaviour

Jumping up, sniffing, or mounting people are amusing actions for a puppy of just about any breed, but not in a full-grown Great Dane or St. Bernard. This can also be deterred with the 'No' response.

If an owner does not want a dog sleeping on the furniture, the 'No' response should again be used. If something more offensive

The Pomeranian has the same prehistoric origins as all the spitz–type dogs, but the breed was developed in the Prussian region of Pomerania.

The popularity of the chow chow dates back to the nineteenth century, when it was taken to England from the East by English merchant ships and given to the Prince of Wales, the future Edward VII.

The poodle is descended from a now nearly extinct French water dog, the barbet. More than most other dogs, it can understand the meaning of the spoken word.

is desired, aluminium foil under a blanket on the forbidden furniture may be more of a deterrent.

Most dogs go through a chewing phase as puppies and can be deterred with a 'No' and taking the object until they outgrow the habit. But if a dog continues this habit into adulthood, it may need to be watched more closely.

It's natural for wild canine puppies to beg for food from their elders, but begging in a human pack is considered by many to be a social faux pas. A simple 'No' or 'Down' should suffice, but other measures, like keeping the dog in another room during mealtime or giving it its own food at dinnertime, might be required.

Commands

There are also some commands that most dogs are expected to know.

'Heel' means the dog walks directly by your side, not ahead of or behind you. Point to the ground at your preferred side.

'Sit' should produce an immediate reaction when you say it and point over the dog's head and at its behind.

'Lay' is easy for a dog to learn from a sitting position; pat the floor in front of the dog and gently pull its front legs forward if necessary to demonstrate.

'Stay' should be said once as you walk away from the dog, and you should eventually be able to walk outside of the dog's field of vision.

'Come' means walk directly to you; it helps if you point to the floor or gently pat your chest as you say it.

'No', of course, is helpful when you want the dog to stop doing something it shouldn't be doing or as a warning not to touch something. It helps to point to the dog or the object.

'Release' means the dog should give up from its jaws (or even its paws) whatever object it is guarding. This is an important command if there are children in the house and shared toys.

The Shar–Pei gives the impression of being slightly sad, but it is happy to live in the home.

The bulldog breathes loudly and snores and is uncomfortable in the heat. Because of the broad head of the breed, puppies need to be delivered by Caesarean section.

COMMUNICATION

While those commands rule dog's interaction with humans, dogs also have rules about their interaction with other dogs. The canines of the world express themselves in a code of a complex of signs, perceptions, and odours that allows them to understand each other. If you watch closely, you might be able to pick up on some of the signals yourself.

When they meet, they have the ritual of pricking up their ears, wagging their tails, sniffing, and barking. (Dogs that have a high proportion of wolf blood are less likely to fight among themselves but are always ready to attack others.)

If the other dog is a friendly member of the same pack, they do the 'wolf greeting', licking and nipping at each other's noses. This explains why dogs like to kiss humans when they see them.

Barking is what most people think of when the subject of dog communication comes up. Most dogs do this to alert the leaders of the pack or to express pleasure at play. But if a dog barks in response to a command, it is probably trying to show its dominance.

Growling is more aggressive and should be taken as a warning to stop or keep your distance. It's true that a growling dog is more dangerous than one that is barking. A lot of growling could mean that your dog considers itself to be in charge of the pack.

Dogs also know that whimpering or whining can be a means to get what they want. Howling is an expression of unity and is used by wild canines to call members of the pack together after they have been separated.

Like humans, dogs also communicate through a variety of body signals—body stance, tail position, facial expression, and ear placement. A dog that lies on its back, exposing its stomach, is submissive. So is a dog who can't look you in the eye too long; so beware of one who dares to stare at you, especially if it is growling.

When a dog gives you its paw without

The Australian cattle dog was obtained principally by crosses between the collie and the dingo. It has a habit of biting at the heels of cows (and people).

Because of the silkiness of its coat, the afghan hound has been called 'a greyhound in pajamas'.

The bearded collie is probably related to the bobtail. It prefers sleeping outside.

prompting, it may be asking for something. This action is instinctive in dogs, as they learned early on that kneading their mother's teats stimulated the flow of milk. As adults, this becomes a begging gesture. This explains why it's so easy for most dogs to learn to 'shake'.

A wagging tail is mistaken by most to mean the dog is happy, but actually it is a sign of indecision. However, if it is accompanied by a happy facial expression, then it is probably a sign of joy.

If the tail is extended horizontally, it indicates contentment; if sticking up, excitement or alertness; if lower between the legs, fear, insecurity, or tension.

Lowered ears show preoccupation and fear; pricked, attention; forward, alarm.

The first traces of a dog similar to the basenji are found in Egyptian tombs and wall drawings of five thousand years ago. Also called the Congo dog, it was brought to Europe in 1934.

The American cocker spaniel is descended through careful breeding from the English cocker spaniel.

The West Highland white terrier originated in Argyll, a former county of west Scotland, when a breeder got some white pups in his litters of cairn terriers. Originally bred for hunting, it is now a popular companion dog.

The puli was brought into Hungary by Oriental nomads around the year 1000. It is very similar to the Tibetan terrier. It loves the water, and it is likely that in past centuries it was used for hunting in marshy areas.

The otter hound is a rather old breed obtained from crossings among the rough–haired terrier, the harrier, the Griffon Nivernais, and the blood-hound. The otter, as the breed's name suggests, is this dog's preferred prey.

Materials and paintings from the sixth century show a dog resembling a small lion. In the seventeenth century, dogs were brought from Tibet and bred in the Forbidden City of Peking. From these dogs the Shih Tzu was developed.

The Chinese crested dog is a little–known hairless breed, probably from Turkey.

TERRITORY

A more subtle way, at least to us, that dogs communicate with each other is by marking territory. When you take your dog out for its daily walks, it may stop at ten or twenty places and make you wonder why the dog can't just urinate all in one spot. Male dogs are more prone to this than female dogs.

Although urination may seem like a simple matter to humans, to dogs it is most serious. Leaving their scent at critical points in the area, as well as scratching at trees, is the way canines mark their territory.

This marking is a signal to other dogs that this particular territory is taken and should not be trespassed. Once the territory is established, the dog will do whatever it must to defend it. Most often this is manifested by barking and growling.

Considering that most wolves' territories are 100 miles (160 kilometres) or more, is it any wonder that dogs get a little riled when the postal service worker steps on the front porch?

NEED FOR PLAY

While dogs are seemingly uptight about their territories, they also have a fun side and enjoy, as well as need, periods of play in their lives.

In the wild, play is used by canines to learn the skills they need for their most important survival skill—hunting. Gearing up for roughhousing, racing with the kids, catching a ball, and tugging on an object––these are things that in the wild would translate into stalking, chasing, attacking, and finally tearing apart the prey.

In domestication, dogs don't need these skills, but they do need to get the instinct to rehearse them out of their systems. Lack of play can cause aggression and maybe even psychological disturbances, so it's important to set aside time each day to play with your dog, even after it reaches adulthood.

The bichon frise was derived from the Maltese in the fifteenth century. It is bold, lively, dignified, intelligent, and affectionate with a strong temperament.

The keeshond is a beautiful Dutch breed with a luxurious coat.

The Akita Inu is native to the island of Honshu in the region of Akita in Japan, where it has remained unchanged for centuries. It almost became extinct because of its use as a fighting dog.

MATING

Something else that may affect your dog's behaviour is its mating instincts. The bitch goes into heat every six months, but it is advisable to wait until the second or third heat before mating so the uterus will have reached adult proportions. The ideal age for the first mating of a male is a year and a half.

Sexual stimulus is always present in males and is aroused by the secretions from the female when she is in heat. The attraction is caused by sexual hormones produced in the testicles and ovaries.

The best time to mate is at the end of the second week of heat, when ovulation is complete. It should be repeated after twenty-four to forty-eight hours. Fertility weakens with age and is lost first by the female and then the male.

The gestation period is sixty to sixty-five days and generally produces four to six puppies, or up to twelve, depending on the breed.

A dog goes through stages not unlike as human being: childhood, teenage, adulthood, and old age. A dog generally reaches adulthood early in the first year, then may compare to human age twenty-four by the second year, forty by the fifth year, and sixty-five by the tenth year.

The Bedlington terrier was developed around 1825 by English miners who wanted a dog that could exterminate the rats in their workplace. The breed, named after a small town in England, was obtained by crossings among the Dandie Dinmont, the otter hound, and the whippet.

Tibet was home to the Lhasa apso, named for the sacred city of Lhasa. It is a hardy dog with excellent hearing and will give good early warning at the approach of strangers.

The Anatolian shepherd dog is an ancient breed native to Asia Minor. It is also known as the Turkish guard dog and was introduced into the United States in 1968.

The Pyrenean mountain dog is probably the strongest of all dogs, but its gentle nature has made it very popular. Its forebears came from Asia more than one thousand years ago, but for centuries they were confined to the Pyrenees, where they were used as sheepdogs.

While dogs are willing workers, they also need periods of play in their lives, as with this Old English sheepdog.

PHOTO CREDITS

INDEX BY PAGE

Page #	Photographer
3	Ron Kimball
4	Kent & Donna Dannen
5	Sally Anne Thompson/Animal Photography
6 (top)	Ron Kimball
6 (bottom)	Ron Kimball
7	Norvia Behling
8–9	Sally Anne Thompson/Animal Photography
10	Sally Anne Thompson/Animal Photography
11	Kent & Donna Dannen
12 (top)	Kent & Donna Dannen
12 (bottom)	S.C. Bisserot/Nature Photographers
13	Sally Anne Thompson/Animal Photography
14	Sally Anne Thompson/Animal Photography
15	Sally Anne Thompson/Animal Photography
16	Sally Anne Thompson/Animal Photography
17	R. Willbie/Animal Photography
18 (top)	Ron Kimball
18 (bottom)	Diane Calkins/Click
19	Kent & Donna Dannen
20	Daniel J. Cox
21	Daniel J. Cox
22	Sally Anne Thompson/Animal Photography
23	Sally Anne Thompson/Animal Photography
24–25	Sally Anne Thompson/Animal Photography
26	Sally Anne Thompson/Animal Photography
27	Sally Anne Thompson/Animal Photography
28	Ron Kimball
29	Sally Anne Thompson/Animal Photography
30 (top)	Ron Kimball
30 (bottom)	Ron Kimball
31	Ron Kimball
32	Sally Anne Thompson/Animal Photography
33	Sally Anne Thompson/Animal Photography
34 (top)	Sally Anne Thompson/Animal Photography
34 (bottom)	Sally Anne Thompson/Animal Photography
35	Ron Kimball
36 (top)	Ron Kimball
36 (bottom)	Sally Anne Thompson/Animal Photography
37	R. Willbie/Animal Photography
38	R. Willbie/Animal Photography
39	Norvia Behling
40–41	Sally Anne Thompson/Animal Photography
42	Sally Anne Thompson/Animal Photography
43	R. Willbie/Animal Photography
44	Kent & Donna Dannen
45	Kent & Donna Dannen
46	Kent & Donna Dannen
47 (top)	John W. Warden
47 (bottom)	Kent & Donna Dannen
48	Ron Kimball
49	Sally Anne Thompson/Animal Photography
50	Sally Anne Thompson/Animal Photography
51 (top)	Ron Kimball
51 (bottom)	Sally Anne Thompson/Animal Photography
52	Ron Kimball
53 (top)	Gay Bumgarner/Photo/Nats
53 (bottom)	Ron Kimball
54 (top)	Sally Anne Thompson/Animal Photography
54 (bottom)	Sally Anne Thompson/Animal Photography
55 (top)	R. Willbie/Animal Photography
55 (bottom)	R. Willbie/Animal Photography
56	Kent & Donna Dannen
56–57	Sally Anne Thompson/Animal Photography
58	E.A Janes/Nature Photographers Ltd.
59	Norvia Behling
60 (top)	Ron Kimball
60 (bottom)	Ron Kimball
61 (top)	Ron Kimball
61 (bottom)	R. Willbie/Animal Photography
62 (top)	Ron Kimball
62 (bottom)	Ron Kimball
63	Ron Kimball
64 (top)	Sally Anne Thompson/Animal Photography
64 (bottom)	Sally Anne Thompson/Animal Photography
65 (top)	Norvia Behling
65 (bottom)	Ron Kimball
66 (top)	Ron Kimball
66 (bottom)	Ron Kimball
67	Ron Kimball
68	Sally Anne Thompson/Animal Photography
69	Sally Anne Thompson/Animal Photography
70 (top)	Sally Anne Thompson/Animal Photography
70 (bottom)	Sally Anne Thompson/Animal Photography
71	R. Willbie/Animal Photography
72–73	Sally Anne Thompson/Animal Photography
73 (top)	Sally Anne Thompson/Animal Photography
73 (bottom)	Sally Anne Thompson/Animal Photography
74 (top)	Sally Anne Thompson/Animal Photography
74 (bottom)	Sally Anne Thompson/Animal Photography
75 (top)	Ron Kimball
75 (bottom)	R. Willbie/Animal Photography
76	Sally Anne Thompson/Animal Photography
77 (top)	R. Willbie/Animal Photography
77 (bottom)	R. Willbie/Animal Photography
78 (top)	Sally Anne Thompson/Animal Photography
78 (bottom)	Sally Anne Thompson/Animal Photography
79	R. Willbie/Animal Photography

INDEX BY PHOTOGRAPHER

Photographer / Page Number

Norvia Behling 7, 39, 59, 65 (top)

S.C Bisserot/Nature Photographers Ltd. 12 (bottom)

Gay Bumgarner/Photo/Nats 53 (top)

Diane Calkins/Click 18 (bottom)

Daniel J. Cox 20, 21

Kent & Donna Dannen 4, 11, 12 (top), 19, 44, 45, 46, 47 (bottom), 56

E.A Janes/Nature Photographers Ltd. 58

Ron Kimball 3, 6 (top & bottom), 18 (top), 28, 30 (top & bottom), 31, 35, 36 (top), 48, 51 (top), 52, 53 (bottom), 60 (top & bottom), 61 (top), 62 (top & bottom), 63, 65 (bottom), 66 (top & bottom), 67, 75 (top)

Sally Anne Thompson/Animal Photography 5, 8–9, 10, 13, 14, 15, 16, 22, 23, 24–25, 26, 27, 29, 32, 33, 34 (top & bottom), 36 (bottom), 40–41, 42, 49, 50, 51 (bottom), 54 (top & bottom), 56–57, 64 (top & bottom), 68, 69, 70 (top & bottom), 72–73, 73 (top & bottom), 74 (top & bottom), 76, 78 (top & bottom)

John W. Warden 47 (top)

R. Willbie/Animal Photography 17, 37, 38, 43, 55 (top & bottom), 61 (bottom), 71, 75 (bottom), 77 (top & bottom), 79